Kennedy's Children

A PLAY IN TWO ACTS

by Robert Patrick

SAMUEL FRENCH, INC.

25 West 45th Street   NEW YORK 10036
7623 Sunset Boulevard   HOLLYWOOD 90046
LONDON   TORONTO

OPENING NIGHT NOVEMBER 3, 1975

J O H N G O L D E N T H E A T R E

————

MICHAEL HARVEY

in association with ROBERT COLBY

presents

KENNEDY'S CHILDREN

a new play by

ROBERT PATRICK

with

SHIRLEY KNIGHT   KAIULANI LEE

BARBARA MONTGOMERY DON PARKER

MICHAEL SACKS   DOUGLAS TRAVIS

Designed by   *Lighting Designed by*
SANTO LOQUASTO   MARTIN ARONSTEIN

Associate Producer
RAMON GETZOV

Directed by
CLIVE DONNER

CAST
(*In Order of Appearance*)

WANDA .... *Barbara Montgomery*

BARTENDER .... *Douglas Travis*

SPARGER .... *Don Parker*

MARK .... *Michael Sacks*

RONA .... *Kaiulani Lee*

CARLA .... *Shirley Knight*

The action of the play takes place in a bar on the lower East Side of New York, on a rainy February afternoon in 1974.

Kennedy's Children

ACT ONE

In the darkness, we hear a RADIO ANNOUNCER'S *voice.*

ANNOUNCER. I think the Presidential motorcade must be approaching now, because the cheers are growing nearer. It's a beautiful day here in Dallas, despite a light rain, and the people have turned out by the thousands to welcome their leader. President Kennedy's political enemies warned that there would be hostilities and riots, but listen to those cheers! Yes, here is the motorcade, and there's the President's car; we can tell because you can see Mrs. Kennedy's pink dress. They've left the bubbletop off the limousine in spite of the rain, so they can see the people, and the people can see them, and they *love* them!

(CROWD *noises are suddenly drowned out by two sharp gunshots. Silence. The lights come up on the interior of an American bar. It is afternoon. Through the barred window we can see that it is raining. The street outside is empty and grim. We see a delapidated warehouse and a filling station. The bar itself is clean, modern, neither very lush nor very low. Theatrical people and their audiences come here at night, so the walls are littered with gaudy posters and handbills for experimental plays: bright, strong images suggesting Pop-art, protest against war and pollution, transvestitism, drugs, sado-masochism, and sex. The posters are in layers; one should be reminded by this of how many plays there are, how few make it, how many people try to get their images of life across. There is a long bar, several stools, a few isolated tables,*

5

a door bearing the sign "Ladies Left, Gents Right,"
another leading to the street. There is a jukebox
which is not turned on until evening, a great, dark,
inert machine. There should be a pay-phone on
the wall. Huge racks filled with bottles of wine
and whiskey fill the wall behind the bar; the after-
noon light slanting through them gives an unreal,
shrine-like feeling to the stage.)

WANDA. For me, it was the most important day of
my life. I measure everything as happening before it,
or after it. I remember every detail, every instant,
every little bit of information as it came in. I was—at
my desk. It was—lunchtime. The executives had gone
out. I was in a hurry to finish page—44!—of the—
May-June issue of 'Salon Hair Styles.' Oh, not that I
wrote it or edited it or anything. I just pasted the
captions to the photos before they sent it out to the
press. It *was* an exacting job though; I had to be very
neat. One time I smeared some glue, and when we got
the covers back for the January-February issue, the
model on the cover looked like she had a runny nose.
But, anyway, I was pasting up these photos, and the
Fashions Editor kept interrupting me to show me her
real Chanel suit from Paris—and I had to pretend to
be interested because she drank something awful—I
didn't drink in those days—and she was lifting up her
skirt to show me how the hemline was kept in place
with little chains sewn into the hem—and all I was
really thinking about was my raspberry yogurt in the
cooler section of the water fountain—and I had just
had this horrible affair with this fellow who worked in
the stockroom—and he hadn't shown up for four days
—I was feeling really awful. (*She looks out the window*
at the rain.) And I remember, it was a grey, grey day
here in New York. And then—all of a sudden—all of a
sudden Mr. Kanowsky, the Advertising Sales Manager,
came bursting in! He was a little cross-eyed and

always looked crazy. Anyway, he came bursting in, red-faced and excited, and he said, "Quick! Turn the radio on! The President's been shot in Dallas!"

SPARGER. I don't know why I come in here afternoons. All my underground theatrical friends come in at night. Oh, right; *that's* why I come in the afternoons. I hate bars. I get sexy in bars. At least *I* think so. Alcohol is otherwise a down. Let's see—I could play a record, but after a while they all look alike. If I were *bi*-sexual, I could go out onto the street and *buy* sex. But look, it's raining! (*Uninterrupted.*) I don't suppose since the creation of the world, it's rained at this particular spot more than a couple of trillion times. And to think that *I'm* here to witness the trillion-and-first! (*The* BARTENDER *sets* SPARGER's *drink down noisily. Uninterrupted.*) What, me? An award? (*Picks up the drink and pretends to read an inscription from it.*) 'For being the trillion-and-first mortal to pass over the bridge from boredom to schizophrenia?' (*Suddenly turning mock-bitch.*) Take those goddamned bars off the window, you creeps. Otherwise we'll never lure any fresh victims in here!

WANDA. Well, none of us believed it. I mean, none of us could conceive it. We just sat looking at him, and I guess we thought he was drunk or having palpitations—he was awful fat—and he said "Did you hear me? Turn on the radio!" So Carrie, the Accounts Payable lady, said, "Now cool it, Mr. Kanowsky, I'll turn the radio on," and he got a little frantic and said terrible things to her, and the Fashions Editor said a couple of unpleasant things to him, and they were squabbling with each other right across me, and then Carrie's radio started up and the newscaster was saying—oh, I want to get this just right—saying, " . . . reported that three Negroes were seen running from the overpass and two rifles have been confiscated in the immediate area," and how the President was going to be all right because they got him right to the hospital, and the Dallas Police were throwing a cordon around the entire area. And then suddenly we couldn't hear any more, because outside it seemed that every auto horn in the city had started blowing, and there was even a crash like somebody had driven right off the street onto the sidewalk, and the phones in the office began to ring—every one of them, all at once, instantly, began to ring!

SPARGER. I'm doing these things with Siamese dancing now, over at the Dada. You know the Dada? It's a rather well-known underground theatre. It's the most famous one, as a matter of fact. Of course, that doesn't make it one-millionth as famous as any chick with her tits and clit spread out in the centerfold of a fuckbook. But, in this tiny little shrivelling, shrinking, curdling clot of snot called "theatre," El Dada is the most famous of the four hundred and twelve underground theatres listed in the 'Village Voice' this week. Which means that if you're lucky enough to work there for a week, you might pull out with a fast five dollars and play to a house of twelve. Twelve: that's the number of people, their average age, and the total of their I.Q.'s.

(MARK *enters, grabs a beer, swallows a pill, washes it down, then sits and takes a briefcase from his duffle-bag.*)

RONA. (*Enters.*) I hate this bar. I wish there was somewhere else to go. I come here day after day and I sit here, *drinking* for Christ's sake. I don't know what else to do. I went ten years without being in a bar, the whole sixties. I mean, I was active then. Now I really don't know what I'm doing. I have these terrible fights with my husband—Robbie—and I wind up here. We're both working, when he isn't shooting up, and we're trying to save enough money to get a commune trip together. But people are so scared. He's scared. I come

in here and I spend all our money and I can't even
seem to get drunk. And half the time I wind up going
home with some black boy. I don't want you to mis-
understand that; I don't think that black boys are
sexier than white men or anything like that. But there
are so few straight white boys anymore—and they can
mostly take their pick of the younger girls . . . I'm
twenty nine.

MARK. (*Reading from letter.*) Dear Mom, believe it
or not, I'm writing to you on pot, Marijuana, what
they call pot. "Whew." I can't believe it. Everybody
here smokes it. The M.P.'s even stand guard on it, and
my buddy, Chick, says he even goes into combat high.
I don't see how they do it. I can hardly even write.
But they do it. All the time. I keep falling down and
they all keep laughing at me and I got very scared at
first. I thought they were all members of some secret
society. I thought the Viet Cong turned them on. Chick
says a lot of people get ideas like that at first, but he
says he—and a lot of others—have been pot-smokers,
or "heads" as they call it, for a long, long time, I'm
scared of being caught. But the weird thing is, I'm
even more scared of my buddies. They have been
trained to fight and kill. So have I, of course—but
they're giggling and dancing and carrying on. I'm more
scared of them than I ever am in action. I'm more
scared of them than I am of the Cong. I don't know
what I'm thinking about; I can't send you *this*.

SPARGER. (*Answers phone.*) Hello. Phebe's. Rehearsal
was cancelled tonight. (*Hangs up.*) I was afraid of
that. I should always take roles in several things at
once; then you're covered. I'm an actor. I'm used to
acting out other people's fantasies. Got any fantasies?
Are they completely cast? Oh. You're waiting for a
friend. Has he got a friend? Only you. (*Sigh.*) Look,
let's be modern about this. It's nineteen seventy four.
Valentine's Day, nineteen hundred, seventy and four.
Look, could I come home with the two of you? I've

always wanted to have sex between two consenting adults.

MARK. (*Reads from his diary.*) Mom. *Dear* Mom. I'm writing this diary for you of things that I can't say in letters. Chick says that writing it all down will be helpful in straightening out my head. I'm down at the beach with Chick and all the other fellas, dancing. You should see us, dozens of us in our underwear, dancing on the beach, making little fires to cook our fish. I'm having experiences I never would have had back home. Your little boy is growing up, Mom. In many ways, this war is a wonderful experience. Oh, I don't mean that I enjoy it; I think one would have to be a sadist or a masochist to enjoy war. Although I suppose in a way those qualities would be very useful in actual time of war. If there was some way to turn them off. Although if we could turn them off, I suppose there wouldn't be any war. If we could turn them off in everyone at once. But I *mean* that I seem to be becoming aware, to be recognizing some of the influences in my life, to *understand* myself. Chick—Chick is a writer, Mom, a kind of person I always, would you believe it?, used to distrust—Chick says I'm 'getting my head.' He says it's very important not to 'get your head in a bad place.' And I said—and this is my first pot joke, Mom; it's a special kind of humor—I said, "Isn't Viet Nam a bad place to get your head?"

WANDA. We all stayed at the office for the whole rest of the day, right into evening, with nobody working—except Carrie, who didn't have any relatives. The minute you'd hang a phone up, it would ring again, and everybody who called was listening to a different station, and getting a different version, and people from other offices would pop in and tell us what they'd just heard, and one man, a middle-aged, respectable man who ran the *yachting* magazine in the next office, came in bawling, just crying like a baby, crying, "Oh, my God, it's a Communist plot, it's the end of the world!"

And the news kept coming in, and you'd get one picture of the whole situation straight in your mind, and then all of a sudden there would be this new piece of information and it would all change, and somebody would break down crying, and they couldn't find the Vice-President—they thought all the politicians were going to be assassinated and I don't know *what* all. And then, at last, very quickly afterwards, not an hour, I think, although it seemed so much longer, they said the President was out of danger and everything was okay. And then the bells starts ringing, every church bell in New York started ringing, and we knew that he was dead. (*She rises, goes to bar for a refill. After a pause.*) I was the first one to say it. I was washing Lena, the Accounts Receivable girl's face, because she was crying and had smudged ink all over her face, so I was right by her phone when it rang, and I picked her phone up, and it was my mother, saying, "Wanda, come home! He's going to be all right! They just said so!" And the Fashions Editor fell out of her office with this big drunken smile on her face and a bottle in one hand, yelling, "J.F.K.'s gonna pull through!" And *that's* when the bells started ringing. And none of them were Catholic, so they didn't know what it meant, and they were all smiling and grinning like fools, and I said, "He's dead. The President is dead. God rest his soul." (*Returns to her table.*)

RONA. I'm from a little nothing town called Niles, not far from San Francisco? I grew up going to these incredible "Blackboard Jungle" type schools where like ten or twenty percent of the students were on parole? I hated it. My parents fought all the time over money and religion. I had a little brother and sister, but *I* was the reader in the family. When I was just a little kid, I was reading Ginsberg and following Martin Luther King in the South and Castro's revolution in Cuba, and I even lied about my age to join the Students' Peace Union. It was in—1960—when I was fifteen, when they

started the black student sit-in's in the South, and I
thought, "Now it's starting! Now is the time!" And it
was. We marched against Caryl Chessman's execu-
tion—I read a poem I wrote—and we marched against
the House Unamerican Activities, and I was practically
a charter member of the SNCC and the SDS. And we
all got thrown into jail for trying to organize cafeteria
sit-in's in Niles and Oakland, but we got out, and we
went, right off the bat we went, all of us who'd been
jailed, right down to Cuba!

CARLA. (*Entering.*) I'm not interested in the sixties.
I'm not interested in any of these nostalgic eras they're
reviving, to tell you the truth. I mean, what are they
really all about? I keep hearing the faggots I know
saying, "Oh, but New York now is really Berlin in the
thirties again," or, "Carla, darling, buy some ballerina
pumps; if the market takes an upward swing we're
going to *be* back in the fifties!" But we're not, you
know. That's just people trying, so desperately, to find
some— (*Laughs lightly.*) "meaning for their own
time." Well! I don't want to get into anything heavy.
This isn't really the place and that isn't really what I
came for. Besides, I've learned—if I've learned anything—and I think sometimes I have, I think sometimes that I've learned everything—I've learned that
people don't want to hear me talk about ideas. People
don't want to hear me talk at all. (*Turns to face
audience. She is breathtaking.*) People want to look at
me. (*Takes paper flower out of a fresh drink.*) I hate
the goddamned sixties! I hate everything that happened in them and everything that didn't happen, and
I hate what happened to me and what happened to
other people! Does that take care of it? Can we agree
about the sixties? Okay, let's just get that clear. They
were rotten. They started out rotten and they got
worse. I mean! They started out with Marilyn Monroe
dying; how good could they get? Well. That's when
they started for me. And look at it out there . . .

raining. I don't think the seventies are going to be any
kind of overwhelming heaven, either, if you want to
know what I think. In fact, if you want to know what
I think—and I know you don't—but even if you don't
want to know—*because* even if you don't want to
know what people think, the sad fact is they're going
to go right on thinking it anyway—what I, me, Carla,
me Carla, what I personally, deep down in my own
unsubdivided, living, pulsing, throbbing, bloody, real,
unknown, unknowable, uncared-for, and utterly un-
important consciousness think—is that the seventies
are just the garbage of the sixties!

SPARGER. (*To imaginary boy.*) My name's Sparger!
What's yours? Oh, have you? Why, yes, I've done a
number of things this year. Maybe you've seen my
name on the wall back there, on some of those stun-
ningly mimeographed flyers for underground theatrical
events of interest to the discriminating theatregoer.
Let us see— (*Looking for the various flyers on the
walls.*) I started out the year playing the fixed star
Regulus in an astrological Halloween pageant in an
abandoned garage, and then I—what's that? Oh, I
always start the year with Halloween; I'm a realist—
and then I did a really well-received improvised sym-
phony concert underwater at the YWHA, and then I
had a really busy week. At eight o'clock I was the left
thumb in a group sensitivity demonstration called
"Hands Off" at the Merrymount Episcopal Community
Center, and then at ten I played a movie projector with
a twinkle-bulb in my mouth in a drag production of
"Bonnie and Clyde" at the Mass Dramatists' Experimental Tavern, and then at the stroke of midnight I
was the cathectic focus of a rather tedious telepathic
theatre event in the basement of the Yoga Institute.
(*Cannot find flyer.*) Oh, right, that one wasn't adver-
tised. We all just sat together and tried to draw Clive
Barnes to us with the power of prayer. I try to keep
busy.

RONA. We—that's Robbie and me— We— That's always Robbie and me, we met in Cuba. We spent most of 1961 in Alabama, doing Freedom Rides and voter registration, and we had to learn about passive resistance, believe me. It was hard for Robbie, him being middle-class and all; he wanted to fight back. When the Southern pigs would come at us, we'd curl up in the passive resistance position and—it was hard for him. When they'd hit me, he'd start to uncurl, and I'd yell, "No, Robbie! Remember what Gandhi said!" Because we read all the Indian philosophy together. We got beat for protesting the Bay of Pigs, and Patrice Lamumba's assassination—we got thrown out of the U.N. for that one, and they beat us—right up against that wall with the quote from Isaiah about "Beating your swords into plowshares?"—They beat *us*. We were right in front; you can see us in photographs in the *Times*, and we stayed in New York for the protest against bomb shelters. For that, they mostly photographed Norman Mailer—but we were there.

WANDA. Within a few hours—do you remember this? —within a few hours one of the major magazines had a special edition out on the newsstands, and of course, within a few days they all did. Mr. Kanowsky ran around and bought everything, every paper, every magazine, he tape-recorded the radio stations, he even ran down—as soon as they announced the President was dead—he ran down and bought a color TV set— just ran down and came right back up carrying it. Puffing and red-faced. And we all watched—but it was all just chaos. Mr. Kanowsky has it all in scrapbooks, everything, all the rumors and confusions, and then all the—you know—Oswald stuff—and all the conflicting reports—and he was even taping from the TV later— he didn't go home for three days—he was even taping the TV soundtrack—when Ruby—did that awful thing. When he sealed the truth off from us forever by firing a single shot—the lips of the one man who might have told us all about it, closed forever by one single little bullet shot . . . or was it two?

CARLA. I wanted to be a sex goddess. And you can laugh all you want to. The joke is on me, whether you laugh or not. I wanted to be one—one of *them*. They used to laugh at Marilyn when she said she didn't want to be a sex-goddess, she wanted to be a human being. And now they laugh at me when I say, "I don't want to be a human being; I want to be a sex-goddess." That shows you right there that something has changed, doesn't it? Rita, Ava, Lana, Marlene, Marilyn—I wanted to *be* one of them. I remember the morning my friend came in and told us all that Marilyn had died. And all the boys were stunned, rigid, literally, as they realized what had left us. I mean, if the world couldn't support Marilyn Monroe, then wasn't something desperately wrong? And we spent the rest of the goddamned sixties finding out what it was. We were all living together, me and these three gay boys that adopted me when I ran away, in this loft on East Fifth Street, before it became dropout heaven—before anyone even said "dropout"—way back when "commune" was still a verb? We were all—old-movie buffs, sex-mad—you know, the *early* sixties. And then my friend, this sweet little queen, he came in and he passed out tranquilizers to everyone, and told us all to sit down, and we thought he was just going to tell us there was a Mae West double feature on somewhere—and he said—he said—he said—"Marilyn Monroe died last night"—and all the boys were stunned—but I—I felt something sudden and cold in my solar plexus, and I knew then what I wanted to do with my life. I wanted to be the next one. I wanted to be the next one to stand radiant and perfected before the race of man, to shed the luminosity of my beloved countenance over the struggles and aspirations of my pitiful subjects. I wanted to *give* meaning to my own time, to be the unattainable luring love that drives men on, the angel of light, the golden flower, the best of the universe made womankind, the living sacrifice, the end! *Shit!*

SPARGER. (*To imaginary boy.*) When this Siamese dancing thing is over—if it doesn't make Broadway— I'm supposed to tour fourteen widely-distributed colleges with an all-male musical of "Lysistrata"—in Lebanese dialect. Unless I get cast in the Amphetamine Theatre's new production of the Third World War. It might be smart to get into that; I think the Third World War is coming back. The only thing is, they don't want us to be in anything else for the entire rehearsal period of two years. Still, it would be something to do, and that's the important thing. If I don't get into something really time-consuming pretty soon, my liver is going to wind up inflammable—like a plum pudding. Alcohol is supposed to kill brain-cells. The trouble is, it's not selective enough. It doesn't necessarily get the right ones.

RONA. By 1962, people were beginning to say the word "student" with fear? European visitors told us how students had always been a political force in Europe—but we were the first like that in America. We were something terrifically exciting and frightening. We were America's big chance for change—*everybody's* chance for change. On the national level, you'd have things happening like the Cuban missile crisis, when for the first time, Americans ran through their big cities with the skies full of police helicopters, afraid of real—not science-fiction—but real, possible, immediate attack. It seemed they had to wake up. And for me—us—personally, it was the time when Robbie and I went to Harvard and learned about L.S.D. For the first time, Robbie saw clearly how society is just a structured game that sucks the individual up for its own uses. I think until then he'd been just doing things for me, y'know? But acid freed him, and allowed him to enlist himself fully for the cause. We were married— really married—by Leary himself. Oh, that was the great time of drugs, the time when they were breaking the chains of lies and prejudice and television over Robbie's mind—over both our minds—over everybody's minds. Hallucinogens showed us how we contained the seed of all things, good *and* evil, within ourselves, and helped us to decide to make ourselves forces for good!

MARK. Mom! If I'm going to write these things I really should be writing them in the sand for the sea to wash away, because I'm very, very afraid of this diary being found. But I want to have it for later, the changes in my head are happening so fast that I want to keep track of them. But words don't seem to go fast enough. That letter I mailed you today was full of lies—no, not lies, it just can't tell you what it's like! That TV news you saw me on—that was a little village, one of dozens we've—liberated—and you should see the natives getting all their possessions into a bundle in just minutes, and then pile the bundle on their heads and run through the streets whenever we— or the Cong—start closing in. They should be pretty good at evacuating by now, I guess, because it is important to remember—It is! *Very* important to remember!—that this little country—arbitrary division on the map—has been the battleground for ten thousand years for every culture that has ever arisen to dominate the world. That is why it is so important that the United Nations finish the job this time, so that we can put an end to war!

WANDA. I couldn't go on working in that kind of job any more, after it happened. I remember the next night, walking along Broadway, and how weird it was to see the theatres all closed—and all these hundreds of color photographs of J.F.K. in the store windows. Somebody must have made a fortune selling those photographs because they were everywhere instantly— or maybe people had had them all along and you just didn't notice them. It was like—like the sun had begun to eclipse. Everyone was scared of a chain of assassinations, or a war, but by the next day, nobody was afraid any more. That had passed, and it had become just—disbelief. In Saint Patrick's cathedral—or outside it, I never got in, the crowds were so big—hundreds of thousands of people were saying prayers for him. The whole world had loved him, you see, so much. The entire human race went into mourning. Kings and queens came to his funeral. All the TV channels had the same things on for four whole days. They even gave us the day off to watch.

CARLA. I wanted to be beautiful. I was. I am. I wanted to be kind. I don't think I've ever been anything less. I wanted to be fun. You tell me. I dress well. I have a good figure. I have a witty little line of polite chat that nevertheless never fails to reveal a terrible vulnerability underneath. And I'm smart. I had before me the whole chart of Marilyn's mistakes. I could guide myself by her and avoid the pitfalls that befell her. I had it knocked. I could even act. I knew writers, painters, photographers. I was liberated. I liked men. I liked a couple of them a lot. I knew how to— manipulate them. I set out with a ruthless plan to do men good. There was only one thing I failed to take into account—if you want to know what I think. And that was that, what with the various film journals, movie magazines, news-wire services, television documentaries, re-release facilities, celebrity postcards, calendars, and endorsement ads, memorabilia shops, movie still collectors, fan clubs, scrapbook keepers, pin-up enthusiasts, gossip columnists, biographers, and original soundtrack recordings, there were about fifty million people exactly like me. Fifty million little media-manufactured racial subconsciousnesses that had systematically, for at least my fifteen years of earthly existence, been subjected, as nearly as conglomerate marketing practices could swing it, to precisely the same arrogant, idealistic input as I. And the day after Marilyn died, fifty million little boys and girls rose up with one overweaning, overwhelming, irresistible, indefatigable ambition: to be the next Marilyn Monroe. And every dirty old man, cross-eyed agent, horny hairdresser, fingerfucking photographer, plastic playwright, demented director, urgent acting teacher, many-handed manager, oral office boy, anal choreographer, phallic vocal coach, orgiastic dress designer, and every other form of unlaid, opportunistic, scaly, slimy, sleazy son of a bitch in this nation's great metropolitan casting centers, suddenly, found him—or her—or themselves deluged under ten million tons of automated, undulating, available, eager MEAT!

SPARGER. (*To imaginary boy.*) Fucking rain. I knew a boy once who could count raindrops. He said. Nobody could refute him on that. He was director. He had the audience enter one show crawling on all fours and when they got into the pitch-black theatre, they were hit in the face with a big sack full of . . . but you probably saw it. Yes, I was in it. I think. I'm not sure. I don't know. I can't remember. I've been in so many shows now where the audience crawled in on all fours and got hit in the face with a big sack of—something. He inspired confidence, though—this boy. The raindrop watcher. Of course, anyone can nowadays. People are so ready to believe anything you tell them. For instance, if I were to tell you I wasn't always like this, you'd probably believe me, wouldn't you? My God, you *would?* But only on condition that I'm willing to believe that you weren't always the way *you* are? Okay, it's a deal. I believe you were different once. I believe everything was different once. I believe it was all the same once too. After all, you've got to believe in something, now that the underground is just an echo chamber and the flower children have all turned into fruits.

RONA. Down South, in nineteen sixty-three, we didn't feel alone anymore because we could hear our own music, Dylan and all the blessed others, starting to happen. We were, all the young, reaching out to each other through wild, crazy, means like that: the top ten charts, and our hair, and the way we dressed. I got taken for Dylan once. And the other side knew something was happening, but they couldn't figure out what. They fired Leary from Harvard, and they killed Kennedy, but they couldn't stop what'd started. Boys began evading the draft, a lot, and we all became aware of that mindless horror going on under *our* name in Viet Nam! And we marched! For peace and civil rights and everything we marched. I don't know how many marches we were on. We'd hitchhike or take busses and trucks and travel anywhere to march. In blazing summer cities, blinded by flashbulbs, we'd walk, chilled by a wind *we* made by walking, a river of long-haired heads rippling down all the avenues, and between the flashbulbs we'd see blue! policemen and black! policedogs and green! soldiers and grey, grey faces. And we'd wave at the faces with the free hand that wasn't helping hold a banner. And we'd read the slogans on the banners backwards from the sun shining through: "WAR MORE NO!" "PEOPLE THE TO POWER!" and "ONE ALL ARE WE!" And we'd ripple and roll that river into the centers of tremendous towns, and there, in blinking lights around the tops of famous towers, letters of flashbulb fire said: "MILLIONS MARCH!"

MARK. Mom! I want to tell you about war, things nobody ever says about it. I understand war, now. I have to do it in this diary because they read our mail, and besides, I think the beach may be bugged. See, we have these men hiding in the jungle waiting to kill us. Well, so have they, of course, they have us waiting to kill them. Because we *have* invaded their country. But we were only trying to get earlier invaders out. But they were only trying to get still earlier invaders out. I don't know where it started. I don't know where it ends. I—I got mad tonight and kicked over the little temple one of the fellas was building out of seashells in the sand. I said, "You killed a man today, Buster, I saw you. You ran him through with your bayonet and kicked him under the philodenderon like my mother has back home. You can't kill a man in the morning and then spend the evening building little seashell temples in the sand. And I wanted to fight. I *wanted* to fight! I WANTED TO FIGHT! . . . But then I couldn't. Fighting is so awful. Chick! Chick gave me a Librium and talked to me until I calmed down. Chick is—*wow!*—wonderful, Mom. He laughs when I say it, but he is my spiritual advisor. I'm getting very spiritual, Mom. Chick is turning me on to Oriental religion.

SPARGER. (*To imaginary boy.*) Naw, I don't get confused rehearsing for a lot of things at once. When I *get* confused is when I don't have any rehearsals to go to—like now. I start drinking, looking around for somebody to get into—as it were. Naw, I can work twenty-four hours a day if I have to, and still come out looking good. I always come out looking good, no matter what piece of shit I'm in. Yeh, they're all shit. You liked it? You liked the one last week, the one with the big spitting scene? You liked that, huh? Tell me, did you read the review before you saw it? The one that said it was "symbolic of things that couldn't be expressed any other way?" I figured you had. Look, would you mind moving away? If I'm going to talk to a brick wall I'd rather talk to a real one. I'm phoney enough for two. I said fuck off, freak! You think because you buy me a drink you can bore me? You could have bored me just as much without buying me the drink! More, in fact! *Move on!* I'd rather sleep with myself. I'd rather not sleep at all than sleep with you. I'd rather talk to myself, anyway. (*Looks around. Boy has disappeared. Sheepishly.*) Oh, right; I am.

WANDA. It's ridiculous to talk about an event like

that from the point of view of somebody like me. I mean, what difference does it make in the long run how I felt about it? I used my savings to finish another year at CCNY—that's City College of New York— enough so that now I have my temporary teaching certificate and can work as a substitute teacher. I just thought—if all of us who believed in him don't go out and try to do some good, then his death was completely—completely in vain. Oh, of course I'm not comparing my little contribution to what he might have done if he had lived. If he had lived, he would have stopped the war. If he had lived, he would have solved the race problem. If he had lived, he would have found some way to bring us all together. I know that there are people who are cynical who say he didn't accomplish much in those—"Thousand Days"—but I always say to people like that, I say (*With mounting anger.*) "Oh, yes? Yes? Yes? Oh, yes? And exactly what have *you* accomplished?"

CARLA. I threw myself, at fifteen, with a sense of mission so strong it would have made Joan of Arc's look like a whim, I threw myself into Manhattan's lap—head first. I bought a subscription to *Show Business* and a subscription to *Backstage* and I borrowed fifteen cents for the subway and I went to all the casting calls. There were an awful lot of pretty girls in New York then. We'd all line up, all pert and prettified, and do whatever we were told to do, like good bad little girls. "Stand up straight." "Swell your chests." "Smile." "Look left." "Look right." And I'd look left and I'd see the backs of the heads of a lot of pretty girls looking left. And I'd look right and see the backs of the heads of a lot of pretty girls looking right. So, I got a job as a go-go girl at the Metropole. We still wore bras then. I had resume photographs made and sent them out to all the important agents. I met an awful lot of important agents. I went out with

several of them—once. I kept abreast of the very latest
styles. I found a guy who'd do my hair for free if I'd
do a number with him in the back of his shop. Only
we weren't yet calling it "doing a number." We called
it "pussycatting." We were—what *was* that word? Oh,
yes—"swingers." He was young and cute. I was young
and cute. It was an exchange of favors. It was also an
exchange of favors with the guy who supplied me with
hats. And—why not admit it?—with the woman who
gave me jewelry. We were young professionals helping
each other. Those people were getting an awful lot of
that kind of help from girls like me. And we were
getting very professional. Well! I never walked the
streets. And I never worked a bar. And I never rode
around Times Square in a taxicab wearing nothing but
a mink coat. Although they'd probably welcome that
as a return to good breeding, compared with the junkies
who are doing the Times Square whoring nowadays.
Because that's what we were—rolled-up copy of *Backstage* or not—*whores!* How do you think I got that job
at the Metropole? Through character references?

SPARGER. The fact of the matter is, I *wasn't* always
like this. Maybe people just weren't meant to live in
the present. Meant? By whom? Who cares? Sure, I
used to live in the present. According to science we all
used to live underwater, too. But we adapted! We just
haven't adapted to the present yet. Not till we grow
asbestos filters in our nostrils. And learn to live on
monosodium glutumate. And survive six inches of steel
shoved up us in every other doorway. And ignore the
pangs of dread and empathy and guilt that *paralyze*
us whenever we see some human being, reduced to a
lump of mucus, come wobbling towards us with his
ragged, flaking hand held out, muttering and blubbering and slobbering, "Help me! Help me! Help me!
For God's sake, somebody please help me!" Uh-oh. I'm
thinking about things I don't want to think about. I'm

too drunk too early. I'm trying to stay off drugs. I haven't got anything left to stop up the back of my brain and I'm having a memory hemmorhage! I'm remembering it all again! I'm remembering! I'm having an attack of the truth! It's coming at me, and it *is* me, the truth, I'm sitting here in a public place, seeping and sopping and soaking and reeking with truth. And the end—the end of truth—is *death!* (*He runs off urgently to the gents'*.)

MARK. Dear Buddha. The Cong I killed today had in his pockets—which I searched, for nothing must be wasted, right? The *man* I killed today had in his pockets a tiny little red lacquered capsule, Buddha— and in it, what do you think he had? You whom they call the All-Knowing One, what do you think he had in his pocket, Buddha? What do you think he also rolls into a little paper cylinder or sifts into a pipe and burns and inhales into his lungs before *he* can come into battle against *me*, All-Seeing, All-Forgiving, Omnipotent, Omniscient Buddha? Which I should have known, which I should have seen, but in order to find out which, I had to propel a ragged atom of burning metal into his irreplaceable heart. And kill him? And *loot his body?* Buddha! Must men die so that other men can see that all men are truly the same? Must each man kill a man before he can see that other men are only men like him and no man must kill? Wasn't Christ enough? Huh? If everybody has to kill a man before he can see that all men are one, then finally all men *will* be one, because there'll only be one man left! And then will *that* man be saved? Do we for God's sake all have to be tortured and robbed and exploited and *die* so that one last man can finally be saved?

RONA. The Black Rebellion, of course, was all that really seemed to matter in 1964. There were the riots in Harlem and Robbie called his mother in Wisconsin and said could we come there because New York looked dangerous. And she said, sure—if he'd cut his hair. I mean, by her he could die if his hair was the wrong length. So we went to my family in Niles, and my little sister took one look at us and ran screaming into a corner of their mobile home, and I said, "What's wrong?" and she said, "You're hippies, you'll hurt me," and I said, "Hippies—" (I hate that *word!*) "Hippies don't hurt people," and she said, "Yes, they do; I see them on the television all the time fighting with the police!" I *mean!* It didn't seem possible, but the same thing was happening to millions of us. Our own parents were saying to us, "Knuckle under or die. In the streets. Alone." And we started to learn what love really meant. It meant caring for one another, literally, feeding and clothing and sheltering one another. People were living together wherever they could, in tenements and lofts and basements. There started being soup kitchens in some cities, and free stores. Robbie was very upset. He got into this really male, paranoid, militaristic thing about how the underground was being infiltrated by FBI and CIA men . . . but I—I was into making music to go with my poetry, a good vibrations trip. I started spending a lot of my time on my clothes and jewelry, lots of people were, it was a movement, things like that, fads and signals would just happen cross country. It was as if a wave of love and beauty was everywhere, growing and becoming strong. The Free Speech Movement arose—I marched—and life itself was like a march to the new music that was sweeping the world now, not just from America but from England, too, the young of the *world* were uniting under the flag of individual freedom. And they were going to tell us what to do with our lives? Sell us to a system? Tell us what we could take into our bodies, even? We showed them! Robbie and I were pushing speed on the streets at the lowest possible prices—and working part-time in a People's Drug

Rehabilitation Center, too. We were building our own counter-culture. It looked as if, maybe, at last, right here on this planet, and right in our own lifetime—civilization had finally begun!

END OF ACT ONE

ACT TWO

SPARGER *re-enters from the gents', shaken and pale. He takes his coat, throws some money on the bar. The* BARTENDER *takes the money, totals* SPARGER'S *tab, rings it up, hands* SPARGER *his change.* SPARGER *starts toward the exit. Suddenly he turns and speaks defiantly.*

SPARGER. The truth is that I used to know a place that was better. It was a little hole-in-the-wall West Village coffeehouse called the Opera Buffo. We did plays. We made a living by peddling coffee and pastries and greasy sandwiches, and twice a night we did plays. We. I was one of us. Them. There. Then. The Buffo! It was the first place that did that, the first place where we got together and did plays without worrying about whether we were going to be a hit, or get a review, or become a star, or take it to Broadway, or get a grant, or anything else in God's forsaken gonorrhea-green underworld except whether we wanted to do it. We got away with it by calling it a coffeehouse, but what it was—was a temple. I was sixteen—and I was bleeding. I was naked from the waist down. Three sailors had picked me up on the New Jersey Turnpike and when they found out I wasn't a real girl, they got tough. I was a mixed-up kid. They mixed me up a little more. They tore off my skirt and worked me over with my Scarlett O'Hara cork-sole wedgies and left me face down on a Greenwich Village side-street— on a set of rusty mattress springs. I don't think I could ever have gotten up if I hadn't heard this *music.* Some dippy music, classical music—opera! Opera, it was. I was shaken and sick and my lower lip was torn by the mattress springs, and I was covered with blood

27

and shit and come, and I thought I'd lost my left eye and at first I thought I was hearing offstage death music like some Tennessee Williams character, and I wanted to get up and run for it, but first I had to *get* up, and then I *was* up, and I could blurrily see cars and people passing at both ends of this one-block long side-street—and the only thing I could think of was this old gay bum that used to hang out behind a diner where I come from in Jersey, and how, if we kids would give him a cigarette butt he'd cackle and tell us about his shock therapy at Bellevue, only he couldn't pronounce the "B" and the "V" and it would come out "Wellewue," and I realized that *that's* what they'd do to me if they caught me staggering around half-naked and I saw this cop's silhouette at one end of the street like a penguin piggy-bank, and I started dragging myself along the street like an alligator, groveling toward that *music*—some soprano cracking the top of her skull with high notes and pretty soon I reached a dreary doorway where I could stand, and I was by then, believe me, in no shape for the senior prom. I couldn't breathe, for instance, and I thought it was all over until I discovered that the sailors had left two poppers shoved up my nose, which was where most of the blood was coming from, and I sneezed those out so I could breathe a little, and, well, what the hell, death was better than Wellewue any way I figured it, so I took a parody of a deep breath and then I kept on crawling down the colorful West Village walls toward that looping, soaring *sound*—because now I had a goal in life: to reach that joint and stop that infernal screeching. So! Half-stripped! And bleeding at the ass like Dylan Thomas! In my taupe turban with the wooden grapes rattling! I trailed gore right up that ditzy damned street until I stood, wavering, in front of this—unlikely!—place with the name "Opera Buffo" across the front doors in green-and-gold glitter. And I

fell against the doors, and the doors fell open, and I
would have fallen, too, if my turban hadn't got caught
in a mobile hanging over the entrance. So there I was,
clawing at my hair and yelping, and then these
shadowy figures at the rear of this empty, insane
coffeehouse stood up and started towards me—and
there were these little flickering little ice-cream lights
everywhere, and the walls were layers deep in magazine pages and movie posters and classical reproduction
—and the people were dressed like a circus clown, and
one like something out of the Hitler Youth Movement, with this glittering necklace of swastikas, and
another like a Romany Gypsy—and on this little stage
in the middle a blonde girl like Botticelli's Venus was
doing a dance with a quadruple amputee—and I
thought I had *flipped*. But then the circus clown,
Buffo, came into the light—and he had this little
bristly beard and the biggest eyes you ever saw—and
he said, in this atrociously phony Italian accent,
"Start-a da show again, Bambini; we hooked-a customer!" And I screamed, "Stop the goddamned music!
Stop it!" And he saw what I looked like and he
yelled, "Stop-a da Casta Diva? Dat's-a not a lady-
like-a way to talk!" By then the Hitler Youth started
freeing my hair from the mobile. And I shrieked at
him, "Listen, lay off the lasagna, gimme some *pants!*"
And then my hair was free and I ran, God knows with
what strength I ran the length of that incredible place
right across the stage I ran, right between the blonde
and the amputee to the record player, and I took that
record, and I smashed it, and I smashed the pieces, and
I danced on them, and then I fell backwards, right into
the arms of the Nazi and the Gypsy and the Corsican
Clown, and on the crumbling ceiling was the James
Montgomery Flagg poster saying, "Uncle Sam Wants
You!" And the clown—Buffo—said, "Mama Mia,
here's another one, and us not making enough to feed

ourselves." Because you see, right then, immediately, he knew, for certain, that I was always—always—going to stay.

WANDA. Looking back to the first time I heard about him—and her—I remember that they had found a way of life we could all imitate. He worked so hard. He was inspiring, encouraging, and of course, so handsome and young—young for a President. And she . . . Well, I was always very fond of her, too. I don't look well, dressed the way she dressed, and I think maybe she let their publicity people—they had their own publicity people, you know—I think maybe she did let those advisors talk her into looking, well, maybe a little less distinguished than she might have looked. The Fashions Editor used to say, before it happened—and even afterwards—she'd look at pictures of Jackie and she'd say, "She looks like a collage of Doris Day's wardrobe, Elizabeth Taylor's makeup, and Natalie Wood's hairdo." I don't think that was kind. I'm sure if she had been a private person, Jackie would have dressed with more restraint and taste. But after all, she was our ambassadrix to the world and I suppose she had to dress in a way that would appeal to people in the mass.

MARK. Mom—this is what I really feel. The world must be one world, Mom. Take my word for it. That is why I continue the war. If I did not, the Viet Cong would overrun the world. I am afraid of their leaders. I am afraid of our leaders, too, but at least I know what their aims are—I think. Chick is helping me. He says, "We must only fight to save our own individual lives and not for any cause." He says, "It is beyond our control." But I am deceiving Chick, Mom. I am fighting for a cause—I am fighting to make the world one. But isn't that what the other side wants? Isn't that what every one of the other sides wants? Maybe it doesn't matter what people believe as long as they all believe the same thing. But what thing? I must finalize which of the available mutually exclusive alternative one worlds I want to make. But in the meantime, I must love everybody, and I must kill the men that come at me every day and night out of the jungle. That is what you say. That is what Chick says. That is what Buddha says when I let him give me a vision. And that is what I say. I don't understand it. I'll do it. I've been doing it. I did it today. I'll keep on doing it. But I don't understand . . . Chick understands.

RONA. In 1965 I saw cops and blacks killing each other on my block in New York, and there wasn't a word of it in the papers! It was up to us to see that people *knew!* We went on the Selma to Montgomery march. I have pictures of us with Dick Gregory and Martin Luther King. Everywhere it started breaking out, we were living our lives in front of television cameras. That was the way to change things. But Robbie got into political reading, and he, and a lot of the cats, and a lot of the chicks, too, were for a violent revolution. But American kids weren't raised for that. They'd start bomb factories and half the time they'd blow themselves up! Besides killing and violence were opposed to the basic message of the Beatles and Donovan and Dylan. Like I said to Robbie—"if you really believe in reincarnation, you want to make the world better—for the next time you come back!"

MARK. We were dancing on the beach when they came at us out of the dark. We were all on mescaline and I thought it was the Cong, but it was the M.P.'s. They flashed lights in our eyes, and beat us, and took us in. I saw them grab Chick, but I didn't interfere. I knew it was wrong to interfere. I should not fight for others. He wasn't fighting for me. Why should he? Or is he a coward? Am I? Has he made me a coward? But we both killed today! Why didn't we kill the M.P.'s and run off into the woods and join the runaway Cong?

Because you can't take sides, right? Right. But then—
what are we still killing Cong in the morning for?

CARLA. There *was* this other thing happening, this
"now" generation, "flower children," "youth rebellion"
bit. I was down here where it was happening, but I had
sort of started this other riff going, you know, the
uptown career bit, and, well, once you start the little
dominoes toppling, it's kind of hard to stop them; you
feel not unlike an idiot. My friends downtown were
doing peace marches and amphetamines—you know—
and I was nightclubbing and first nighting and—sleeping around. I knew an awful lot of people. I really did.
I really *do.* I can pick up the phone and spend the
night with any number of famous people from the
forties and fifties—if I want to. I never went to bed
with anybody for a role—that's true. I never got any
roles, either. I don't say I didn't think of it. In fact,
well, I did, sort of, once. There was this agent. He
wasn't too bad. Well, he was, but I had been doing
this bit in this crummy nightclub, dressed in a se-
quinned corset, introducing the acts on amateur night—
there were a lot of them, too—and this agent had
started wining and dining me. He was—nice. He kept
saying he wanted to help me, but he couldn't cast me
unless I slept with him, because he'd feel *I* was taking
advantage of *his* tender feelings for *me.* So one night
I decided—well—I had a few drinks to work myself
up to it—then a few more, and then we got back to my
place and we had a few more, and then we got into
bed, and I got on top of him, and I leaned over, and
he breathed in my face, and—I—threw—up. (*She goes
politely, if a little unsteadily, off to the ladies'.*)

WANDA. When they were alive—I mean when she
was alive—when *he* was alive, you could never resist
reading about them. He could read a half-dozen books
a day, and he had been a war hero. And, you know, it
was him that popularized the James Bond books. It's
true. They weren't that popular at all until he men-

tioned to a reporter that he liked them and then, well, do you remember how suddenly everyone was reading James Bond? And she was very responsible for starting a certain "look" among young women. Politician's wives since her have all *tried* to dress nicely. And, oh, do you remember that record, "The First Family?" That was so popular. It had all sorts of jokes—good-natured jokes, really—about him and her and his brothers and just everybody. Drugstores and super-markets had stacks of it beside their cash-registers. And he wrote books, too, and one of them won the Pulitzer Prize, really, when he was still just a Senator. And she, when she was still a student, won the Vogue Magazine Prix de Paris for her article on "My Favor-ite Artists I Would Most Like To Have Known From The Past." They were remarkable people! Everything they touched turned to gold!

MARK. They released us. I don't know why. I don't know why they arrested us. I don't know "why" any-thing. But I can answer the question that I asked before. The reason it is all right to kill in battle but not to resist authority like all those misguided pacifists are doing back home is that it is all right to protect yourself but not all right to *take sides.* I know this is what Chick has been trying to tell me all along, al-though he is too smart to talk about it any more, because now they are onto us. I know that he is think-ing that we will have to be very quiet when we go back to the beach. Because we are going back. Because we have to. To stay sane. Right? Right, Mom? Right, Buddha? Right, Chick? Right.

RONA. About nineteen sixty-six, the Lower East Side here started filling up with—insincere kids. They read about the Revolution in *Time* magazine; it was a vacation for them. And the marches would start out as marches *for* something and wind up as *hate* rallies: hate whites, hate soldiers, hate Johnson, hate grape-growers. And kids who weren't used to slums and

ghettoes were overdoing drugs. We left here and went
to San Francisco. Thousands did. We'd made mistakes
in New York, sure, but California was a second chance.
The streets in Haight-Ashbury were a carnival. In-
credibly young people, tripping and digging each other
and dying to live. The Big Be-In, the first be-in they
called a be-in, in 1967—that was the peak.

SPARGER. Buffo was a ballet dancer who got too fat.
So he opened a coffeehouse with the idea that his dance
friends could use a place to congregate. Well, he picked
such a dumb location that nobody came. He couldn't
go home—you're not supposed to be a Sicilian *and*
a ballerina—so his Family kept the place going to keep
him out of sight. Anyway, after I made my ungainly
entrance, Buffo found a Red Cross Nurse outfit and
made the Hitler Youth number wear it to take care of
me. Except Corso, the Hitler Youth, changed the Red
Cross to a swastika. Well, nothing that I needed very
badly was broken, so I was on my feet in a week, and
Buffo swore that I'd be "tap-a dancing" again, which
was a joke, because his favorite people were the
Rockettes. But I secretly studied tap from a twenty-
five cent Fred Astaire secondhand paperback, and one
night, before the nine o'clock show, I announced to
three N.Y.U. students and a Caribbean astrologer that
there would be a brief prologue that evening, and I
signalled Corso to put on "Mack the Knife," and then
I proceeded to do my two time-steps alternately for
fifteen minutes. Biting my tongue. Well, the audience
was understandably transfixed, but Buffo, when he
came out of shock, ran on stage and announced that
next week I would do the "full-a four-hour version."
Then he hit me in the face with a pie. I poured ketchup
over his head. He slapped me in the face with a raw
fish. I tap-danced on his toes. He went on point and
pirouetted. The blonde and the amputee got tired of
waiting and came onstage and went into *their* dance.
We weren't about to stop, so Buffo let me have it with

every insult in the "operatic-a-reper-a-tory," and I countered with every wisecrack I remembered from four million Glenda Farrell musicals. And, as fate would have it, a critic from the Village Voice was there that night—looking for deaf-mute boys—and he wrote us up that week as the latest thing in Dray-mah. And the next thing we knew, we had to hire a waiter! The reviewers came back and then we had to hire a dishwasher, who had to be a frustrated set-designer, and a host, who had revolutionary ideas in costuming, lighting, and menu layout. And somewhere in there the middle sixties must have passed, because I think it was in nineteen sixty-six when I had a day off—in the hospital—that I realized there were one hundred and twenty-five underground theatres listed in the papers, that three of our playwrights had books coming out, and one was on Broadway, and one had a TV show, and another had bleeding ulcers—that was me—and that was the only time I had off in all those years, because right about then, the piranhas, yes the piranhas, right about then the piranhas moved in.

WANDA. He *was* from a wealthy family, of course, but they had made their money themselves, and they were still, you know, rough, charming, brawling Irishmen, whereas she was from very "old money" as they call it, and she would have been a career girl, a photographer, if they hadn't met. They were so happy. They loved that musical "Camelot," the story of a distant, beautiful, forgotten kingdom where there was always sunshine and justice. Camelot. "Don't let it be forgot, That once there was a spot, For one brief shining moment, That was known as Camelot." Camelot. I think maybe we all had a glimpse of Camelot—once—just once—in our own lifetime—before it crumbled.

MARK. Two Cong came out of the sea onto our beach, Buddha, or whoever you are. They came out of the darkness in little wet loincloths. They gave me pot in those little lacquered capsules. We gave them some of ours. We smiled at one another and walked arm in arm along the beach. We showed them our great sea-shell temple. Not a word was said. We will kill them in the morning if we must. And they will us. I do not hate them nor, I feel, do they hate me, but you cannot tell another's feelings. There is no way to know. They slipped back into the sea. And they disappeared.

RONA. I get 1967 and 1968 confused. There was the Pentagon march—Robbie spent a month afterwards sitting in a corner, muttering to himself—"Stick flowers in their rifles."—They jailed Huey Newton, they shot Martin and Bobby—they murdered those three black students, the cops beat down the May rebellion in Paris—France—drugs turned into big business—and all these cults grew up—gurus and prophets and Allah and Jesus—and everybody quarreling over religion and money—San Francisco got to be just awful, just a junkie slum after the summer of peace and love—we left San Francisco and came to New York, to get ready for the Democratic Convention in Chicago—only now everywhere you went these famous writers—Mailer and Ginsberg and William Burroughs—who I thought was God—and Jean Genet, and all of them, all of them writing about everything like it was some sort of romantic epic. I mean, people died in Chicago, baby—people you never heard about—they herded us around with guns and billy clubs and mace—I think the mace was in Chicago—I went through a plate glass window—but I was all right—but Robbie took one look at me lying there in the broken glass and this awful look came over his face—and he and his gang grabbed the cops' billy-clubs and they fought back. And they really hurt him—them—(*Screams.*) No!—I would never call a cop again for anything—anything ever. Not that they did anything if you did call them, not in the neighborhoods we lived in. Nothing. Nothing—except beat up girls and steal dope.

CARLA. (*Re-entering, a little vague.*) What kept me

sane all this time was something I'd do when I was alone. I'd bathe, slowly, in bath-oil—scented bath-oil. Then I'd wash and condition and dry my hair and get it all fluffy and lovely. And I'd dust myself dry with a perfumed dusting powder. And I'd do my nails, hand and foot, with a clear—a lovely, subtle, clear nail-polish. And then I'd dress myself, slowly, in these things I never, ever, wore anywhere else. Underwear—no, lingerie—that was all pink and black lace—and stockings of silk—not nylon at all, but silk, dark and seamless, very expensive. And a gown that looked heavy with glitter but actually was lovely and light and clinging. And then this boa that I'd gone crazy for and worked extra shifts at the Metropole to get, a huge downy soft white number that enfolded me like a cloud. And I'd stand before the mirror and remind myself of just what it was I wanted to do: the heart as big as the known world; the moon glowing to fullness within me; my great liquid eyes like the great southwestern skies; my flesh delicious as the petals of tender little flowers; my lips dark, precious, unique, the black rose . . . People were complaining that you couldn't tell one of the girls in the movies from another one, they all looked alike. Ursula Andress warmed-over. And then you started hearing talk that the studios were doing it deliberately, that after the troubles they'd had with Kim Novak and Marilyn and Elizabeth Taylor and all of them, that they didn't *want* any more movie stars, no more crazy actresses to demand huge salaries, that they didn't care which woman they used, that nobody cared, because all the audiences wanted was just one supergirl after another, that the mini-skirt mattered more than the girl, that James Bond didn't care who he fucked, because they were all alike! And I guess, if they felt like that about them, then *they* all were.

WANDA. They made "Camelot" into a movie, but it wasn't really very—I mean, it was just a medieval

pageant, it didn't have the tenderness and the beauty
and the sense of—you know—something that could
really happen. And it was—you know—very sexy—
really dirty, for a musical. I didn't watch the second
half at all. People don't seem to—I would have thought
there would have been a lot of letters in the newspapers
about it—about them messing up the President's
favorite musical. But there weren't. I guess people had
forgotten *little* things like that. In fact—when you
walk down on Orchard Street, the pushcart street down
in the Village where you can buy a lot of things cheap?
Well, one time I was down there after some movie
actress died—I don't even remember her name, although my mother was quite broken up about it—and
they had replaced all the pictures of him with pictures
of her. It was—horrible. You know how stores have
the pictures in the frames they're trying to sell? I
mean it's the frames they're trying to sell, not the
pictures? Well, instead of having him in the frames,
or even him and Bobby Kennedy and Martin Luther
King—they had these pin-up photos of the girl who
had just died. Just because—well, not for any *reason!*
Just because she had *died!* I mean people seem to
remember, they seem to care, but they seem to have
gotten things all mixed up.

SPARGER. The Buffo had been started by rejects,
nomads, exiles, rebels, outcasts. So now that the estab-
lishment critics had started selling the place on that
basis, we started drawing the real rot: the junkies and
the psychopaths. We never needed critics before—we
sold sandwiches! And now more and more we attracted
not the real rebels, or the real dropouts, but failures
and phonies from uptown who just wanted to do whatever had been original and daring the year before. The
new phony audience read the reviews and *loved* us!
But for us, the sanctity, the privacy, was gone. There
was no other reward; the amount of work was un-

speakable. Oh, and then I found out that Buffo and the others, who I'd worshipped for their energy and originality and brilliance and verve, had just been on speed all those years, while I'd worn myself out learning to keep up with them. But Buffo started getting into heavier drugs, letting his junkie friends put on *that* kind of show—at the Buffo. He was so tired. We all were exhausted, like sea creatures swept up on the beach by the tide, cut off from the element of their life. No. More like sea creatures helpless to *leave* their element, while it's slowly being poisoned by settling grime and *muck!*

WANDA. You hear stories now—and I don't mean just the stories about how it wasn't really Oswald who killed him, but it was really Johnson, or it was really Nixon, or Cubans, or oil millionaires, or Communists, or Ruby, or all of them together—*or* how the avant-garde threatre people put on all those awful parodies of Shakespeare—*or* how the sincere Shakespeare people in the park revived anything that had the killing of a king in it. I think some of those people mean well, but it sure is funny how they all do seem to be making a buck out of it—isn't it? No, I mean that you hear stories that make you wonder just how well people remember. I mean stories like—that Jackie was paid a million dollars to stay with him because they really hated each other. Or that they were both homosexual. Or that he had a movie-actress mistress. Or that he was in the pay of big industry, or—things that nobody could know, anyway, even if they were true. And you wonder: why do people even want to speculate about such things? When there's so much good to remember? When, above all, the beauty that never even got to happen is still there, waiting for us all to build! What right have they got to talk against her? How can they blame her for getting married again? My God, just to get away from all the people that try to make her into some kind of a pin-up girl, or clown! When she was there! Right there beside him! Closer than anybody in the world!

MARK. I think Chick is in league with the Viet Cong. It all came to me last night. It is a very subtle plan. All that pot, all that talk, getting everyone down to the beach? A time will come when we will be attacked by groups of false M.P.'s who are under Chick's command and we will all be driven down into the sea where we will be picked up by giant Viet Cong submarines and transformed by plastic surgery into indistinguishable Cong soldiers! *That* is where they get their unending supply of troops! *That* is the truth behind the treasonable rumors of desertion from our own forces! Chick, and a few more like him, are in the pay of the Viet Cong! . . . I could be wrong; they may be in the pay of the Soviet Russians. I even think I have some evidence that our own government may be behind the whole thing. Yes, the M.P. attacks were to blind us to the fact that it is our own government that is selling us drugs—perhaps—but—it doesn't matter. The important thing is that I am beginning to see *some* pattern in it all. Wait. No. Chick is not in league with anyone. That is insane of me to think so. I have been —innocently—falling prey to the over-rationalistic Western tendency to try to connect everything into one great pattern. Which is wrong, because that is what makes men totalitarianistic. I have also been mistaking my own feelings and fantasies for objective facts. Plus my own natural aggressive tendencies—which I cannot help—have misled me into projecting these territorial power fantasies onto other people. I still believe, in spite of everything, that people are basically good. They do the evil things they do for the same reason that I have these delusions. Because I am evil? But then so are they. But they are not. And I am not either. But someone must be . . . someone . . . someone.

RONA. I made Robbie go to Woodstock. After they sprayed the tear gas on us in the People's Park in Berkley, I had to *make* him go. He wanted to leave for Mexico, he wanted to run away, but when we started getting the vibes about Woodstock, I made him go. Half a million people stood up together to defy what was going down. Robbie just looked at it and said, "Kids. Standing out in the open. They don't know what's happening. They're gonna drop an atom bomb on us." But they didn't. Sure, the media and the press ripped it off for movies and albums, but that's how you work within the system; ya make 'em see what you *are*. Robbie just said, "Let them fight for it now. I've had enough." He was—into heroin. Oh, we'd hear stories about—wonderful things, the priests burning the draft records, the G.I.'s themselves resisting the war! And he'd just say, "Yeah? Yeah? Yeah? Look at the streets." And it was true, it was true, the streets here on the Lower East Side had turned into the same thing as Berkley, just kids, streaming, hungry, diseased, drugged, stealing, hustling, crazy, marks chalked all over their faces, muttering psychedelic, superstitious, pseudoreligious shit! Or black beggars, shivering and snarling. People would come from other countries, saying, "We want to be American; you're where it's at." And how could we tell them we were licked, we were through? We weren't! We aren't . . . When Robbie got better, he campaigned for Nixon; he said it was the quickest way to tear the country down. Every day Robbie was into something new: Hare Krishna or a Catholic monastery—or he was going to be a moviemaker, or weave beads—and then he decided for some reason that Vanessa Redgrave was living next to us disguised as a Puerto Rican and taking tapes of our conversations, and that John Lennon was God, and Mick Jagger was the Devil and Donovan was Christ . . . *CHRIST!* . . . That was the winter of sixty-eight, sixty-nine. That was the winter that produced

"Bridge Over Troubled Water?" and "Let It Be?"
That was how the sixties ended.

CARLA. I guess James Bond really didn't care, because at about this time all the men I knew turned
gay, or were revealed to have been gay all the time,
or maybe they just came out. It was certainly better
than sleeping with Raquel Welch and cutting yourself
on her . . . I don't mean to down her. She did a
terribly difficult thing at a time when it just didn't
pay to be a girl at all. She actually made people think
about her. But it hasn't lasted—apparently. I mean,
no body is that beautiful. And to be that beautiful
takes all one's time, there's no time left to be beautiful
inside, to be human, to be warm or fulfilling. Besides,
all the reviewers prefer the drag queens. It's amazing.
Esquire, last month, this young boy who reviews for
them? He just flipped, he freaked, over these three
famous drag queens, who—get this!—are the fellows
I roomed with in nineteen sixty-two! It's so funny. If
you'd told me at the start of the sixties that the com-
petition would be *drag queens!* Wasn't there supposed
to have been a sexual revolution in there somewhere?
Weren't all the disguises and masks supposed to have
been dropped? I mean! When Raquel Welch and a
bunch of drag queens are the current sex-symbols,
isn't something *wrong?* What made them hate women?
And men? What made them hate men? Is it just
because there are so many people and media and all
have made them so much alike? Is that why everyone
keeps harking back to another era, any other era, any
freak, any monster, anything different? Why don't we
want anything beautiful? Why don't we want anything beautiful to be, to exist, to live? Is it over-
population or what? Are we just instinctually avoiding
reproduction? Stimulation, involvement, reproduction?
Everybody's drunk! Everybody's drugged! Everybody's making TV commercials! There are *no stars!*
What's wrong with them? What's wrong with me?

WANDA. But there are some of us who still try—who still try to go on. My work—I'm going to have a full teaching license in just another three years—I'm working with subnormal—what they *call* subnormal children, out in Jersey. It's very hard to try to help them into the world. They are of minorities, children whom the culture has forgotten, children of twelve who can't speak because they have never been spoken to in their homes, children who are afraid of things they can't even name, children without love or hope. Some of them may never be able to join the human race. But I can try. Today I mentioned to them something—something about him—and not one of them, not a single one of them, even knew who he was. It was, for a moment, as if he had never been. I tried to show them that famous *Life* magazine with the color photos of the—assassination—but it excited one of them too much, and two of the others just went crazy at the pictures of the blood—so, I wound up instead just telling them about Camelot. Without the sex stuff between Guinevere and Lancelot, of course. It's almost the same story. If I'd wanted to, I suppose I could even have told them the story of Christ, and it would have been almost the same story.

MARK. Chick *is* a traitor. I have evidence now. Today we entered a bombed-out village where all the people were dead—except that a single Cong soldier jumped at me from behind a pile of bodies and knocked me down and raised his bayonet over me, prepared to bring it down onto my head—or possibly my neck. And Chick, my teacher, Chick, who was relieving his bladder and should have continued to do so—Chick, *groovy* Chick, turned and shot the Cong in the head and sent him flying away. I got up and I thanked Chick, but he knew, I could tell by the expression on his face and by certain vibrations, that he knew, that I knew, that he has betrayed everything we believed in. Because he *took sides!* At a time when there was no danger to his own individual life, Chick took sides and killed to save mine. Chick is a traitor, Mom . . . and he knows about *you*.

SPARGER. Buffo was away sick or drugged or crazy a lot of the time now, and the new kind of people wouldn't show up to do their shows, and Corso, who was Buffo's lover, couldn't stand it and split. Buffo didn't know who to blame for what was happening. News came that Corso had been killed in a motorcycle accident. Corso's family wouldn't even let Buffo come to the funeral. Buffo would vanish. And there were all these awful vegetable people hanging around. More and more people left. Sometimes, we'd spend all day, two or three of us, getting the place together, scrubbing and shopping, wait tables, wash dishes, improvise a show if one didn't show up, and sleep on the stage, unpaid, waiting for Buffo. And he'd come in, if at all, blubbering and screaming, "Help me! Help me! Help me! For God's sake, somebody please help me!" And then he'd tell us all to go away and throw chairs at us. Finally they all *went* away. I closed up one night and went looking for Buffo. Buffo came back to the Buffo, alone. He put on the "Casta Diva" and locked the gates. He took a hatchet and cut off his hand and tried to cut off his foot. He hacked away at his neck and face, broke two ribs, and then succeeded in cutting his stomach open with forty-four strokes. His guts fell out onto the stage. He had enough strength left to chop up his guts. He lived for four days and died on Corso's birthday. Their parents wouldn't let them be buried together. The critics named an award after him the next year. This is a recording. Wait sixty seconds and leave your message.

CARLA. I won't do what those people do on television, smile and pucker and have an orgasm about floor-wax. I won't be dehumanized and robotized and dance around Dean Martin. I won't pose for the porny magazines. I won't go dyke because I don't want to. I

won't sleep with any more second assistant stage
managers to get an audition as a replacement in a role
after some movie star's niece has already gotten the
reviews! And I *won't* traipse around in the court of a
famous drag queen, hoping for a bit-part in one of
their vehicles. Marilyn wouldn't have. I know that
much. She started late, but she was smart. She knew
when to get out. She started—I mean, really started—
when she was twenty-six. I was twenty-six. Today. I
took seventy-four sleeping pills a little while ago in my
apartment. I just came in here to wash them down.

RONA. The last big march was against the mining of
the harbor at Hanoi, and besides the old chant of
"One-two-three-four, We don't want your fucking
war," my friends were muttering, "Why are we here?
We've been marching since we were babies and all we
did was make Jane Fonda famous." Some people will
tell you it ended when they murdered the students at
Kent State, and everybody left the Village. Or when
the papers played up the drug-cult murders and people
got scared of each other. Or when the pot famine hit
and all the kids got hooked on alcohol. Or when Hair
opened and Abbie Hoffman became a guest-star. Or
when Leary got brainburned and ran away. Or when
the Beatles sued each other. And Donovan retired to
his private island, and Dylan to his million-dollar
farm. Or when Janis and Jimi and Jim died—so young!
—and those were our heroes, the models for our lives!
The men don't understand Women's Lib and the women can't dig Gay Power. The blacks don't need us and
the Indians don't want us. And the new kids are no
use—my sister lives on downers. And my little brother
is a nineteen-fifties fascist! He wrote me, "Fuck the
Revolution! I don't want anything collapsing on me!
I want fifty thousand a year, and when I lose my
looks I'll overdose!" They're selling sixties nostalgia
albums already. The nearest thing to a political cause
is bisexuality. And the streets between here and the

house are just junkies and black bums and rapists. But we did *some* good. We did. They didn't stop the war, but they reduced it. Pornography is legal almost everywhere. They've slowed down their stupid space program. The corruption at the top is blown wide open. And, sure, the people are hungry and tired and weak and disillusioned, but isn't that a sure sign that something's crumbling? I try to tell Robbie that this is the time for action of some kind, the time when leaders are needed, but he just backs! into a corner of this dump! we're living in on a welfare fraud! and waves his fix! at me, and he says, "Sure! Let's fight for peace! Let's fight for freedom! I'm all for it! What do you want me to do? Where do you want me to start? Who do you want me to *kill?* What do you want me to be: Lee Harvey Oswald?"

MARK. (*Puts his letters and diary away, pays his bill, stops at the door.*) We are safe, Mom. Chick is physically dead. They do not check every little battlefield casualty for autopsies. And besides, I used a Cong rifle. My tour of duty is over, Mom. Whoever is actually in charge has decreed that I am to be sent to what they call a Methadon clinic in New York City. What it actually is, I do not know. I must spend some time there being further indoctrinated. But then I will be coming home again, to make the world a better place to live in. Now, I know how. (*He exits.*)

WANDA. And yet, even after they understood the story, it was hard to make them see why it had all been so wonderful. There's no one like that now, they can't even imagine anyone like that, they're used to the idea that the world is just a swamp of violence and crooked politics and unexpected death and ugliness everywhere. They can't understand that there was time, a space of several years, when everyone loved someone, someone bigger and better than other people. They can't understand that all the people—everyone in the world—loved him. All. But one.

(The BARTENDER *looks at his watch, sighs, comes from behind the bar, turns on the jukebox, deposits a coin, makes a selection, turns on the neon sign "Bar" in the window, then hits a light switch and simultaneously the lights blaze, the jukebox blares.* SPARGER *sits staring into space,* WANDA *returns to grading her papers,* RONA *hands her glass to the* BARTENDER *for another drink,* CARLA *lies slumped over the bar, completely ignored. Slowly the curtain falls.)*

THE END OF "KENNEDY'S CHILDREN"

PROPERTY LIST

ACT ONE PRESET
Bar: *Rear Counter Top:*

2½ Gal. Paul Masson Chablis—full—water & food coloring

2½ Gal. Paul Masson Burgundy—⅓ full—Welch's Grape Juice & Water

2 bottles of Vodka with swigger tops—water

2 bottles of Scotch with swigger tops—water and food coloring

1 round bar tray with 2 old fashion glasses

   2 brandy snifters

   2 beer glasses

   2 wine glasses

2 plastic ashtrays

1 notepad

3 sharpened pencils

1 order pad with 6 loose pages

1 quarter

1 cash register set at $1.80

   with drawer with 10 singles

               2 five dollar bills

               3 coins

1 stationary bell next to cash register

1 blender

1 portable television

1 bill stand

1 bar napkin stand with napkins

1 jar of drink stirrers

Rear Shelves:

370 liquor bottles of assorted varieties

8 beer glasses

17 water glasses

15 old fashion glasses

10 brandy glasses

24 champagne glasses

12 cordial glasses

3 theatre flyers

1 day calendar—February 14, 1974

2 metal bar trays

48

1 small liquor ad sign
1 liquor license framed

Counter Top:
Note: Flap open; bar has a rail of brass that protrudes into
    the room
1 Village Voice Newspaper
1 Underground Newspaper
1 old fashion glass with 4 short stem plastic flowers
5 plastic ashtrays
1 glass of toothpicks
1 plastic flower
3 paper bar napkins
1 glass of drink stirrers
1 brandy snifter of white wine
2 protruding beer taps
1 silver tray service area
1 corner shelf—at round corner

Under Counter:
3 pitchers of X-Beer with Frothe Whiskey Sour Mix for Head
1 bucket of ice—large cubes
3 beer glasses
3 old fashion glasses
3 wine glasses
3 brandy snifters
1 bar tray
1 bar towel
1 sponge
1 hand broom
1 hand shovel
1 long spoon
1 pitcher water
1 slop pail
1 waste can
3 safety matches

10 tall barstools–next to bar
1 28″ round black vinyl-top pedestal table (*Down Right*)
    with 1 black plastic ashtray
1 18″ round black vinyl barstool
1 large plastic plant on banquette shelf
1 electric switchplate

1 36″ round black vinyl top pedestal table (*Down Center*)
2 18″ round black vinyl barstools
(*Note: all three of these pieces are secured to the floor permanently*)
1 28″ round black vinyl-top pedestal table (*Up Center*)
2 18″ round black vinyl barstools
1 black plastic ashtray
1 brightly colored jukebox that lights up
1 electric switch box
2 electric neon signs
1 black wall telephone—coin machine with 9′ spiral cord practical in that it must return a coin

Banquette Area (Down Left):
Shelf:
1 ad ashtray
1 large plastic plant on four-legged pedestal
Seat:
1 dark blue lady's raincoat—folded
1 brown leather clutch purse with:
  1 hair brush
  assorted makeup
1 36″ round black vinyl-top pedestal table
1 pair of lady's eyeglasses—horn-rimmed variety
1 old fashion glass with 2 ice cubes
1 black plastic ashtray
1 school pouch with:
  1 12″ ruler
  3 sharpened #2 pencils
  2 sharpened red pencils
  2 sharpened blue pencils
  2 ballpoint pens
12 school notebooks with children's lessons inside
1 teacher's planning book
1 grade book
1 cigarette machine
1 phone book
1 bulletin board with posters etc.
1 pad with scribbling on it

Dressing:
24 theatre posters on ceiling board
assorted posters on wall by bar and behind Banquettes

5 theatre posters above windows upstage
2 electric bathroom signs—1 Men's, 1 Ladies'

Offstage Left Prop Table:
  2 plastic flowers
  1 pack of Marlboro Lights
  3 dimes (sprayed pennies—silver for phone)
  1 box paper clips
  1 package of chewing gum
  1 school notebook
  1 sharpened red pencil
  1 pencil sharpener
  1 plastic water sprayer—full of water
  1 white towel
  1 green army laundry bag—tied end with:
    1 snap lock samsonite attache case with:
      1 manilla envelope with:
        1 tattered written air mail letter (1 piece)
        1 army brochure
        1 Buddha brochure
        assorted newspaper articles and letters
  1 plastic container for pills filled with mints
  1 loose mint
  3 stacks of money:
    3—$10. bills
    2— 5. bills
    6— 1. bills
  1 pitcher of water
  4 empty water glasses
  extra stock pile of money

Personal Props:
WANDA:
1 pendant watch
1 small gold cross on chain

BARTENDER:
1 small white towel on belt attachment
1 wristwatch

MARK:
1 neckchain with 2 small keys (1 fits attache case)

Rona:
1 cloth shoulder bag
1 wallet
1 autograph book
1 cigarette lighter
1 safety matches
Carla:
1 pair large sunglasses
1 tan leather shoulder bag
1 beaded makeup bag
1 compact and mirror with powder puff
1 hairbrush
1 comb
1 lipstick
assorted makeup
kleenex
1 sleek tan lady's umbrella

INTERMISSION—ACT II CHANGE:

Strike:
1 pitcher beer—downright table
1 glass—downright table
empty glasses—bar
1 glass—downleft table
1 vodka glass—bar

New Preset:
1 pitcher fresh beer—bar
1 beer glass—bar
1 glass of red wine—bar
1 clean glass for Carla—bar
1 glass of whiskey for Wanda—bar

Move:
Carla's raincoat—from stool to barcounter
Wanda's purse—from downleft table to bar
Mark's green bag with things—from downright table to bar-stool-leaning
Mark's diary—from downright table to bar counter
Turn Off switch on jukebox

Prop Notes:
  X-BEER is used for beer with Frothe (whiskey sour mix
    used for head) and can be secured from; Canada Dry
    Corp. 59-02 Borden Avenue, Maspeth, N.Y. 11378
Food Coloring Mix for Liquor:
  scotch:
    6 parts yellow
    4 parts red
    1 part green
  chablis:
    1 part yellow
Burgundy:
  ½ water
  ½ Welches Grape Juice
  note: spill grape juice down side of glass to avoid bubbles.

SOUND PLOT

  1 telephone bell
  2 tape recorders
Tech:
  1 cue lite by front door

SOUND CUES

1. Record Speech at top of show with crowd noises and gunshot
2. "Help" by the Beatles—End of ACT ONE.
3. "Yesterday"—Beatles—Top of ACT TWO.
4. "American Pie" by Don McLean—End of ACT TWO.

COSTUME PLOT

WANDA:

    gray long sleeved wool dress
    beige blouse
    brown suede shoes
    pearl earrings
    pin on blouse collar
    gold cross on chain
    watch
    pantyhose
    blue raincoat—preset by property dept.
    blue canvas tote bag—preset
    brown leather clutch bag—preset
    glasses—preset

BARTENDER:

    brown corduroy pants
    orange T-shirt
    blue denim shirt
    brown braided belt
    multicolored socks
    beige suede oxfords
    belt loop with bar towel

SPARGER:

    black qiana knit shirt
    black velour pants
    black socks
    black patent leather shoes
    black raincoat
    silver rings, bracelet and pendant

MARK:

    blue dungarees
    green undershirt
    blue plaid flannel shirt
    green socks
    green army fatigue jacket
    desert boots
    dog tags
    black leather belt

RONA:
blue denim pants with patches
pink knit shirt
brown velvet jacket
tweed socks
brown oxfords
blue wool poncho with belt
green wool shawl
burlap bag
pink and green print scarf
wooden hair clip
beaded necklace
wire and bead bracelets

CARLA:
blue matte jersey dress
beige raincoat
beige and white scarf
beige gloves
beige umbrella
bone shoes
gray pantyhose
white boa
saddle bag
beaded clutch bag
crystal drop on chain
crystal bracelet
crystal earrings
blue glasses

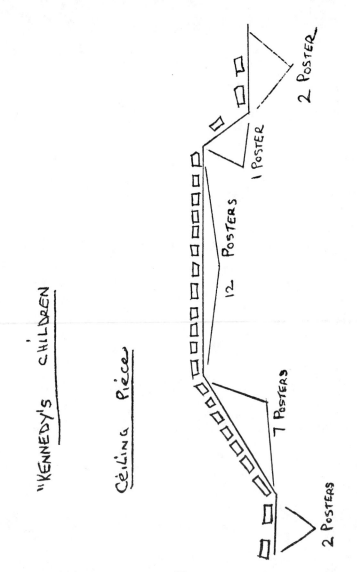

"KENNEDY'S CHILDREN

Ceiling Piece

2 Posters

7 Posters

12 Posters

1 Poster

2 Poster

FLOORPLAN "KENNEDY'S CHILDREN"

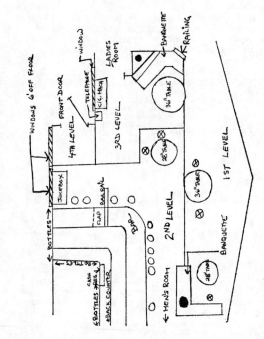

6 RMS RIV VU
BOB RANDALL
(Little Theatre) Comedy
4 Men, 4 Women, Interior

A vacant apartment with a river view is open for inspection by prospective tenants, and among them are a man and a woman who have never met before. They are the last to leave and, when they get ready to depart, they find that the door is locked and they are shut in. Since they are attractive young people, they find each other interesting and the fact that both are happily married adds to their delight of mutual, yet obviously separate interests.

> ". . . a Broadway comedy of fun and class, as cheerful as a rising soufflé. A sprightly, happy comedy of charm and humor. Two people playing out a very vital game of love, an attractive fantasy with a precious tincture of truth to it."—*N.Y. Times.*
> ". . . perfectly charming entertainment, sexy, romantic and funny."—*Women's Wear Daily.*

Royalty, $50—$35

WHO KILLED SANTA CLAUS?
TERENCE FEELY
(All Groups) Thriller
6 Men, 2 Women, Interior

Barbara Love is a popular television 'auntie'. It is Christmas, and a number of men connected with her are coming to a party. Her secretary, Connie, is also there. Before they arrive she is threatened by a disguised voice on her Ansaphone, and is sent a grotesque 'murdered' doll in a coffin, wearing a dress resembling one of her own. She calls the police, and a handsome detective arrives. Shortly afterwards her guests follow. It becomes apparent that one of those guests is planning to kill her. Or is it the strange young man who turns up unexpectedly, claiming to belong to the publicity department, but unknown to any of the others?

> ". . . is a thriller with heaps of suspense, surprises, and nattily cleaver turns and twists . . . Mr. Feeley is technically highly skilled in the artificial range of operations, and his dialogue is brilliantly effective."—The Stage. London.

Royalty, $50—$25

THE SEA HORSE

EDWARD J. MOORE

(Little Theatre) Drama
1 Man, 1 Woman, Interior

It is a play that is, by turns, tender, ribald, funny and suspenseful. Audiences everywhere will take it to their hearts because it is touched with humanity and illuminates with glowing sympathy the complexities of a man-woman relationship. Set in a West Coast waterfront bar, the play is about Harry Bales, a seaman, who, when on shore leave, usually heads for "The Sea Horse," the bar run by Gertrude Blum, the heavy, unsentimental proprietor. Their relationship is purely physical and, as the play begins, they have never confided their private yearnings to each other. But this time Harry has returned with a dream: to buy a charter fishing boat and to have a son by Gertrude. She, in her turn, has made her life one of hard work, by day, and nocturnal love-making; she has encased her heart behind a facade of toughness, utterly devoid of sentimentality, because of a failed marriage. Irwin's play consists in the ritual of "dance" courtship by Harry of Gertrude, as these two outwardly abrasive characters fight, make up, fight again, spin dreams, deflate them, make love and reveal their long locked-up secrets.

"A burst of brilliance!"—*N.Y. Post.* "I was touched close to tears!"—*Village Voice.* "A must! An incredible love story. A beautiful play?"—*Newhouse Newspapers.* "A major new playwright!"—*Variety.*

ROYALTY, $50-$35

THE AU PAIR MAN

HUGH LEONARD

(Little Theatre) Comedy
1 Man, 1 Woman, Interior

The play concerns a rough Irish bill collector named Hartigan, who becomes a love slave and companion to an English lady named Elizabeth, who lives in a cluttered London town house, which looks more like a museum for a British Empire on which the sun has long set. Even the door bell chimes out the national anthem. Hartigan is immediately conscripted into her service in return for which she agrees to teach him how to be a gentleman rather after the fashion of a reverse Pygmalion. The play is a wild one, and is really the never-ending battle between England and Ireland. Produced to critical acclaim at Lincoln Center's Vivian Beaumont Theatre.

ROYALTY, $50-$35

A Breeze from The Gulf

MART CROWLEY

(Little Theatre) Drama

The author of "The Boys in the Band" takes us on a journey back to a small Mississippi town to watch a 15-year-old boy suffer through adolescence to adulthood and success as a writer. His mother is a frilly southern doll who has nothing to fall back on when her beauty fades. She develops headaches and other physical problems, while the asthmatic son turns to dolls and toys at an age when other boys are turning to sports. The traveling father becomes withdrawn, takes to drink; and mother takes to drugs to kill the pain of the remembrances of things past. She eventually ends in an asylum, and the father in his fumbling way tries to tell the son to live the life he must.

> "The boy is plunged into a world of suffering he didn't create. . . . One of the most electrifying plays I've seen in the past few years . . . Scenes boil and hiss . . . The dialogue goes straight to the heart." Reed, Sunday News.

Royalty, $50–$35

ECHOES

N. RICHARD NASH

(All Groups) Drama
2 Men, 1 Woman, Interior

A young man and woman build a low-keyed paradise of happiness within an asylum, only to have it shattered by the intrusion of the outside world. The two characters search, at times agonizingly to determine the difference between illusion and reality. The effort is lightened at times by moments of shared love and "pretend" games, like decorating Christmas trees that are not really there. The theme of love, vulnerable to the surveillances of the asylum, and the ministrations of the psychiatrist, (a non-speaking part) seems as fragile in the constrained setting as it often is in the outside world.

> ". . . even with the tragic, sombre theme there is a note of hope and possible release and the situations presented specifically also have universal applications to give it strong effect . . . intellectual, but charged with emotion."—Reed.

Royalty, $50–$35

VERONICA'S ROOM
IRA LEVIN
(Little Theatre) Mystery
2 Men, 2 Women, Interior

VERONICA'S ROOM is, in the words of one reviewer, "a chew-up-your-finger-nails thriller-chiller" in which "reality and fantasy are entwined in a totally absorbing spider web of who's-doing-what-to-whom." The heroine of the play is 20-year-old Susan Kerner, a Boston University student who, while dining in a restaurant with Larry Eastwood, a young lawyer, is accosted by a charming elderly Irish couple, Maureen and John Mackey (played on Broadway by Eileen Heckart and Arthur Kennedy). These two are overwhelmed by Susan's almost identical resemblance to Veronica Brabissant, a long-dead daughter of the family for whom they work. Susan and Larry accompany the Mackeys to the Brabissant mansion to see a picture of Veronica, and there, in Veronica's room, which has been preserved as a shrine to her memory, Susan is induced to impersonate Veronica for a few minutes in order to solace the only surviving Brabissant, Veronica's addled sister who lives in the past and believes that Veronica is alive and angry with her. "Just say you're not angry with her," Mrs. Mackey instructs Susan. "It'll be such a blessin' for her!" But once Susan is dressed in Veronica's clothes, and Larry has been escorted downstairs by the Mackeys, Susan finds herself locked in the room and locked in the role of Veronica. Or is she really Veronica, in the year 1935, pretending to be an imaginary Susan?

> The play's twists and turns are, in the words of another critic, "like finding yourself trapped in someone else's nightmare," and "the climax is as jarring as it is surprising." "Neat and elegant thriller."—*Village Voice*.

ROYALTY, $50-$35

MY FAT FRIEND
CHARLES LAURENCE
(Little Theatre) Comedy
3 Men, 1 Woman, Interior

Vicky, who runs a bookshop in Hampstead, is a heavyweight. Inevitably she suffers, good-humouredly enough, the slings and arrows of the two characters who share the flat over the shop; a somewhat glum Scottish youth who works in an au pair capacity, and her lodger, a not-so-young homosexual. When a customer—a handsome bronzed man of thirty—seems attracted to her she resolves she will slim by hook or by crook. Aided by her two friends, hard exercise, diet and a graph, she manages to reduce to a stream-lined version of her former self—only to find that it was her rotundity that attracted the handsome book-buyer in the first place. When, on his return, he finds himself confronted by a sylph his disappointment is only too apparent. The newly slim Vicky is left alone once more, to be consoled (up to a point) by her effeminate lodger.

> "My fat Friend is abundant with laughs."—*Times Newsmagazine*. "If you want to laugh go."—*WCBS-TV*.

ROYALTY, $50-$35

PROMENADE, ALL!
DAVID V. ROBISON

(Little Theatre) Comedy
3 Men, 1 Woman, Interior

Four actors play four successive generations of the same family,
as their business grows from manufacturing buttons to a conglomerate of international proportions (in the U.S. their perfume will be
called Belle Nuit; but in Paris, Enchanted Evening). The Broadway
cast included Richard Backus, Anne Jackson, Eli Wallach and Hume
Cronyn. Miss Jackson performed as either mother or grandmother,
as called for; and Cronyn and Wallach alternated as fathers and
grandfathers; with Backus playing all the roles of youth. There are
some excellent cameos to perform, such as the puritanical mother
reading the Bible to her son without realizing the sexual innuendoes;
or the 90-year-old patriarch who is agreeable to trying an experiment
in sexology but is afraid of a heart attack.

"So likeable; jolly and splendidly performed."—*N.Y. Daily
News.* "The author has the ability to write amusing lines, and
there are many of them."—*N.Y. Post.* "Gives strong, lively
actors a chance for some healthy exercise. And what a time
they have at it!"—*CBS-TV.*

ROYALTY, $50-$35

ACCOMMODATIONS
NICK HALL

(Little Theatre) Comedy
2 Men, 2 Women, Interior

Lee Schallert, housewife, feeling she may be missing out on something, leaves her husband, Bob, and her suburban home and moves
into a two-room Greenwich Village apartment with two roommates.
One roommate, Pat, is an aspiring actress, never out of characters
or costumes, but, through an agency mix up, the other roommate
is a serious, young, graduate student—male. The ensuing complica-
tions make a hysterical evening.

"An amusing study of marital and human relations . . . a gem
. . . It ranks as one of the funniest ever staged."—*Labor Her-
ald.* "The audience at Limestone Valley Dinner Theater laughed
at "Accommodations" until it hurt."—*News American.* "Superior
theater, frivolous, perhaps, but nonetheless superior. It is light
comedy at its best."—*The Sun, Baltimore.*

ROYALTY, $50-$25

THE GOOD DOCTOR

NEIL SIMON

(All Groups) Comedy
2 Men, 3 Women. Various settings.

With Christopher Plummer in the role of the Writer, we are introduced to a composite of Neil Simon and Anton Chekhov, from whose short stories Simon adapted the capital vignettes of this collection. Frances Sternhagen played, among other parts, that of a harridan who storms a bank and upbraids the manager for his gout and lack of money. A father takes his son to a house where he will be initiated into the mysteries of sex, only to relent at the last moment, and leave the boy more perplexed than ever. In another sketch a crafty seducer goes to work on a wedded woman, only to realize that the woman has been in command from the first overture. Let us not forget the classic tale of a man who offers to drown himself for three rubles. The stories are droll, the portraits affectionate, the humor infectious, and the fun unending.

> "As smoothly polished a piece of work as we're likely to see all season."—*N.Y. Daily News.* "A great deal of warmth and humor —vaudevillian humor—in his retelling of these Chekhovian tales."—*Newhouse Newspapers.* "There is much fun here . . . Mr. Simon's comic fancy is admirable."—*N.Y. Times.*

(Music available. Write for particulars.)
ROYALTY, $50-$35

The Prisoner of Second Avenue

NEIL SIMON

(All Groups) Comedy
2 Men, 4 Women, Interior

Mel is a well-paid executive of a fancy New York company which has suddenly hit the skids and started to pare the payroll. Anxiety doesn't help; Mel, too, gets the ax. His wife takes a job to tide them over, then she too is sacked. As if this weren't enough, Mel is fighting a losing battle with the very environs of life. Polluted air is killing everything that grows on his terrace; the walls of the high-rise apartment are paper-thin, so that the private lives of a pair of German stewardesses next door are open books to him; the apartment is burgled; and his psychiatrist dies with $23,000 of his money. Mel does the only thing left for him to do: he has a nervous breakdown. It is on recovery that we come to esteem him all the more. For Mel and his wife and people like them have the resilience, and the grit to survive.

> "Now all this, mind you, is presented primarily in humorous terms."—*N.Y. Daily News.* "A gift for taking a grave subject and, without losing sight of its basic seriousness, treating it with hearty but sympathetic humor . . . A talent for writing a wonderfully funny line . . . full of humor and intelligence . . . Fine fun."—*N.Y. Post.* "Creates an atmosphere of casual cataclysm, and everyday urban purgatory of copelessness from which laughter seems to be released like vapor from the city's manholes."—*Time.*

ROYALTY, $50-$35

COUNT DRACULA

TED TILLER

(All Groups) Mystery comedy

7 Men, 2 Women. Interior with Small Inset

1930 Costumes (optional)

Based on Bram Stoker's 19th Century novel, "Dracula." This is a new, witty version of the classic story of a suave vampire whose passion is sinking his teeth into the throats of beautiful young women. Mina, his latest victim, is the ward of Dr. Seward in whose provincial insane asylum the terrifying action transpires. Her finance arrives from London, worried over her strange inertia and trance-like state. Equally concerned is Professor Van Helsing, specialist in rare maladies, who senses the supernatural at work. Added trouble comes from Sybil, Dr. Sewards demented, sherry-tippling sister and from Renfield, a schizophrenic inmate in league with the vampire. But how to trap this ghoul who can transform himself into a bat, materialize from fog, dissolve in mist? There are many surprising but uncomplicated stage effects, mysterious disappearances, secret panels, howling wolves, bats that fly over the audience, an unexpected murder, and magic tricks which include Dracula's vanishing in full view of the spectators.

> Despite much gore, ". . . the play abounds with funny lines. There is nothing in it but entertainment."—*Springfield, Mass. News.*

ROYALTY, $50-$25

FRANKENSTEIN

TIM KELLY

(All Groups)

4 Men, 4 Women, Interior

Victor Frankenstein, a brilliant young scientist, returns to his chateau on the shores of Lake Geneva to escape some terrible pursuer. No one can shake free the dark secret that terrifies him. Not his mother, nor his financee Elizabeth, nor his best friend, Henry Clerval. Even the pleading of a gypsy girl accused of murdering Victor's younger brother falls on deaf ears, for Victor has brought into being a "Creature" made from bits and pieces of the dead! The Creature tracks Victor to his sanctuary to demand a bride to share its loneliness—one as wretched as the Creature itself. Against his better judgment, Victor agrees and soon the household is invaded by murder, despair and terror! The play opens on the wedding night of Victor and Elizabeth, the very time the Creature has sworn to kill the scientist for destroying its intended mate, and ends, weeks later, in a horrific climax of dramatic suspense! In between there is enough macabre humor to relieve the mounting tension. Perhaps the truest adaptation of Mary Shelley's classic yet. Simple to stage and a guaranteed audience pleaser.

ROYALTY, $25.00